# Translating Mo'um

# Translating Mo'um

## Cathy Park Hong

Hanging Loose Press
Brooklyn, New York

Published by Hanging Loose Press, 231 Wyckoff Street, Brooklyn, NY 11217-2208. All rights reserved. No part of this book may be reproduced without the publisher's written permission, except for brief quotations in reviews.

Printed in the United States of America
10 9 8 7 6 5 4 3 2 1

Hanging Loose Press thanks the Literature Program of New York State Council on the Arts for a grant in support of the publication of this book.

Cover design by Jen Liu
Additional design by Pamela Flint

Acknowledgments: Thanks to the editors in which these poems first appeared: *Pushcart Prize 2000*, *Columbia Review*, *Field*, *Hanging Loose* and *Mudfish*. And of course the deepest gratitude to the following: My family, the Van Lier Fellowship, Martha Collins, Sunyoung Lee, David Eng, Ryan Chowdhury, Jen Liu, and to many other friends and teachers who have encouraged me along the way.

Library of Congress Cataloging in Publication information available on request.

ISBN 1-931236-11-9 (paperback)
ISBN 1-931236-12-7 (hardcover)

 Produced at The Print Center, Inc. 225 Varick St., New York, NY 10014, a non-profit facility for literary and arts-related publications. (212) 206-8465

# CONTENTS

## I.

Zoo . . . . . . . . . . . . . . . . . . . . . . . . . . . . . . . . . . . . .13
Ontology of Chang and Eng, The Original Siamese Twins . . . . . . .15
Rite of Passage . . . . . . . . . . . . . . . . . . . . . . . . . . . . . .17
Helix . . . . . . . . . . . . . . . . . . . . . . . . . . . . . . . . . . . . .19
Assiduous Rant . . . . . . . . . . . . . . . . . . . . . . . . . . . . . .20
Translating *Pagaji* . . . . . . . . . . . . . . . . . . . . . . . . . . .21
Scale . . . . . . . . . . . . . . . . . . . . . . . . . . . . . . . . . . . .23
Body Builder . . . . . . . . . . . . . . . . . . . . . . . . . . . . . . .24
Melanin . . . . . . . . . . . . . . . . . . . . . . . . . . . . . . . . . . .25
Assimilation of Sitting . . . . . . . . . . . . . . . . . . . . . . . . .26

## II.

The Shameful Show of Tono Maria . . . . . . . . . . . . . . . . . .31
During Bath . . . . . . . . . . . . . . . . . . . . . . . . . . . . . . . .35
All the Aphrodisiacs . . . . . . . . . . . . . . . . . . . . . . . . . . .37
Not Henry Miller but Mother . . . . . . . . . . . . . . . . . . . .39
On Splitting . . . . . . . . . . . . . . . . . . . . . . . . . . . . . . . .40
Movement . . . . . . . . . . . . . . . . . . . . . . . . . . . . . . . . .43
Translating *Michin'yun* . . . . . . . . . . . . . . . . . . . . . . . .44
To Collage a Beginning . . . . . . . . . . . . . . . . . . . . . . . . .45

## III.

Hottentot Venus . . . . . . . . . . . . . . . . . . . . . . . . . . . . .53
Androgynous Pronoun . . . . . . . . . . . . . . . . . . . . . . . . .57
The Scavenging . . . . . . . . . . . . . . . . . . . . . . . . . . . . . .58
CAT Scan . . . . . . . . . . . . . . . . . . . . . . . . . . . . . . . . . .60
Wing . . . . . . . . . . . . . . . . . . . . . . . . . . . . . . . . . . . . .61
Ablution . . . . . . . . . . . . . . . . . . . . . . . . . . . . . . . . . .65
The Gatherer . . . . . . . . . . . . . . . . . . . . . . . . . . . . . . .67
Translating Mo'um . . . . . . . . . . . . . . . . . . . . . . . . . . .68
Timetable . . . . . . . . . . . . . . . . . . . . . . . . . . . . . . . . .73
Notes . . . . . . . . . . . . . . . . . . . . . . . . . . . . . . . . . . . .74

*To my mother and father*

*The grotesque body....is a body in the act of becoming.
It is never finished, never completed; it is continually
built, created, and builds and creates another body."*
—Mikhail Bakhtin


*She mimics the speaking. That might resemble speech.*
—Theresa Hak Kyung Cha

**I.**

# Zoo

*Ga*     The fishy consonant,
*Na*   The monkey vowel.

*Da*   The immigrant's tongue
       as shrill or guttural.

Overture of my voice like the flash of bats.
The hyena babble and apish libretto.

Piscine skin, unblinking eyes.
Sideshow invites foreigner with the animal hide.

Alveolar *tt*, sibilant *ss*, and glottal *hh*

*shi*:      poem
*kkatchi*:  magpie
*ayi*:      child

Words with an atavistic tail. History's thorax considerably
cracked. The Hottentot click called undeveloped.

Mother and Father obsessed with hygiene:
as if to rid themselves of their old third world smell.

Labial *bs* and palatal *ts*:

*La*   the word
*Ma*  speaks
*Ba*   without you

I dreamed a Korean verse, a past conversation
with Mother when they said I was blathering unintelligibly
in my sleep.

The mute girl with the baboon's face unlearned
her vowels and cycled across a rugged phonetic map.

*Sa*   glossary
*Ah*  din
*Ja*   impossible word

Macaws turned into camouflaged moths.
The sky was overcast, the ocean a slate gray

along the wolf-hued sand. I dived into the ocean
swam across channels to islands without flags;

replaced the jingoist's linotype with my yellowing
canines and shrilled against the anemic angel who

cradled the bells that dictated time and lucid breath.

# Ontology of Chang and Eng, the Original Siamese Twins

Chang spoke / Eng paused.

Chang threw a beach ball / Eng caught it.

Chang told a white lie / Eng got caught for the lie.

Chang forgot his first language / Eng picked up English.

In letters, Chang referred to themselves as "I"/ Eng as "we."

While proselytizing, the preacher asked Chang, "Do you know where you go after you die?" Chang said, "Yes, yes, up dere." / Thinking they didn't understand, he asked, "Do you know where I go after I die?" Eng said, "Yes, yes, down dere."

Chang married Adelaine / Eng married her sister Sally.

Chang made love to his wife / Eng daydreamed about money, his Siam childhood and roast beef. He tried not to get aroused.

Chang checked his watch, scratched his head and fidgeted/
Eng made love to his wife.

Chang became drunk, knocked Eng out with a whiskey bottle and went carousing with his boys / Eng was unconscious.

Chang proved Einstein's time dilation while drunkenly running from one bar to the next / Eng was unconscious.

Chang apologized / Eng grudgingly accepted.

Chang paused / Eng spoke / Chang interrupted.

"I am my own man!" / Eng echoed, "We are men yes."

Both broke their bondage with their pitchman, Mr. Coffin.

Both owned land in North Carolina and forty slaves.

Both were nostalgic for Siam: childhood of preserving
duck eggs, watching tiger and elephant fights with the King,
Mother Nok who loved them equally.

The physicians were surprised to find both were "personable."

Both did not appreciate the outhouse joke.
"Are all Orientals joined?" "Allow me to stick this very sharp pin
in Eng's neck to see if both of you feel the pain." "Is it true that
you turn babies into cabbages?" "We are nice, civilized people.
We offer you bananas."

Both were sick of fascination.

Both woke up, played checkers, sired children, owned whips
for their slaves, shot game, ate pie. Both wore French black silk, smoked
cigars, flirted. Both believed in the tenets of individualism.
Both listed these activities to the jury and cried, "See, we are American!"

Both were released with a $500 fine for assaulting another head hunter.

Both were very self-aware.

Both insisted on an iron casket so that grave robbers would not
dig up their bodies and sell them to the highest bidder.

Both did not converse with one another except towards the end:

"My lips are turning blue, Eng"/ Eng did not answer.

"They want our bodies, Eng." / Eng did not answer.

"Eng, Eng! My lips are turning blue." / Eng turned to his body and did not answer.

# Rite of Passage

Childhood was spent in an open dressing room where
white women pulled chenille over their breasts and

I felt oddly collaged: elbow to nose, shin to eye,
neck to breast, brow to toe

When I flirted, marbles slivered out of my mouth
like amphibious eggs.

*Hey saekshi*, the American GIs cried to the Korean
barmaids, pronouncing *saekshi 'sexy'*

though *saekshi* meant *respectable woman,*
*a woman eligible for marriage.*

The arterial clouds shouldered a glassy reservoir.
Divers made thin sleeves in the water,

Fog rolled over the dry shrub mountains
like air conditioning.

*She's back*, the saleslady whispered to her assistant,
when Mother came to try on a blouse.

A rain of Rapunzels fell from their towers,
bodies first, hair trailing like streamers.

My first kiss was with a twenty-year-old man
who whispered *your hands are shaking.*

When thoughts of disgrace invaded the mind,
I hummed or sang to drown out the noise.

A stutter inflated and reddened the face:
eyes bulged and lips gaped to form,

a fortune cookie cracked and a tongue rolled out.
Wagged the Morse code but no one knew it.

Antidepressants lined up like clever pilgrims.
I felt quiet that night.

Fragments of freaks: the Hottentot's ass,
the Siamese twins' toupee, the indecisive chink

who said, I do. Later, no forget it, I do not.

# Helix

It was a spring when geneticists stole milk bottles
from the stoops of brownstones owned
by art docents who waved their arthritic fists when they saw
those lab-coated Robin Hoods scamper off with their precious dairy.
The bottles were used to house mutant fruit flies,
those beloved atoms of behavior.
It was a spring of many mutations—
I was sent outside the classroom for lack of behavior,
sent back in for good behavior, and sent back out again.
On the way in, I met half a Siamese twin who asked, "And who?"
On the way out, I met the other half who replied, "are you?"
"Lactose intolerant," I said and we all bonded ionically
like salt. Many-limbed children played in the park,
tulips were double jointed. What was my fate?
A Harvard graduate investment banker whose parents
owned a glassed-in liquor store in the Bronx
gave me a palm reading: "Will your own future the way
I willed mine," he said, "That will be $10."
We then haggled about the price, as if we
were in a swap meet and he was selling me a cheap
brand name shirt that smelled of rayon and
faintly, just oh so faintly, of fish.

# Assiduous Rant

Here is a morning when English
is gibberish so *blue* is *blur* or *bliss*;

Mother assembles dolls in the assembly line,
works at a shoe store, then she stops working;

Flowers belie a smooth mitosis in green houses,
the sun is a constant x in the equation of silence;

I draw lopsided gowns and cheer for the giant's death.

When I finally understand English, a classmate cups
her hands around my ear. I am eager for the tender

secret and she screams gibberish in my ear.

'What is this, a Korean parade?' the obese pale man
cries to the ragtag circle of skinned-kneed kids.

I save my words for a cold, indecipherable day.
Think of acidic quips years after the attack.

The source is the gorging mouth, the tale
half-told: the giant was Indian,

The king kidnapped him and had him
macerated for his whale-like bones.

# Translating "*Pagaji*"

*please fill all appropriate blanks with "pagaji."*

Angrily, she turned _____ but said nothing.

In the new country, she wore a Napoleonic jacket
and drank box wine. She was _____to
box wine and

glycerin _____ but was too embarrassed
to tell anyone.

When she did not reach a certain height, she
looked into hormonal _____ though

they said _____ was perfectly average for
Asian women

She felt a bloated sense of cultural _____
so she took some antacids.

She did not _____, she strode.

In college, her shyness was mistranslated as _____,
so to look the part, she acquired pierces.

Was it her Napoleonic jacket? European men with their
Vittel water bottles and blinding Adidas' hounded
her for directions. She told them to _____.

She hollered _____ ! and turned the school into guerilla—

_____ with a straight face. Later they found out that

it was stolen from _____, a dystopic novel.

In the new country, she eventually grew _____
to make up for height.

It became the irrepressible joke. She could affect
any facial _____. But _____ was more
versatile, because of its daredevil

_____ . She grabbed

coupons for eyelid surgery at _____ .

_____ is a plastic container that can be bought
in rainbow hues at your local Korean grocer.

_____ is making love with suit intact, zipper down.

She conquered the cul-de-sac through slash and _____.

In the old country, the old woman wearing a towel over
her head washed scallions in the _____. She
scratched her head scarf. It was a good day.

# Scale

Tigers the size of caviar pounce through fiery
hoops ignited by the flea-sized man.

A girl jerks off in a mouse hole and a serf
naps on a scrap heap of dirty fingernails.

Diasporic curios, glass bells, boxes by Joseph
Cornell, objects of dear privation.

The homunculus escapes from anatomy class,
leaving a trail of detachable organs.

The life-sized airplane is suspended from the ceiling
and underneath, the blind molest the model.

Alone in Europe, I shrank and darted around
chapels and closed glass factories,

And inflated when the Norwegian bartender
offered me free beer, port wine, and his number.

Shapes warped in memory: my cousin's chin
tripled in size, Mother was a giant,

the pastor was a bigger giant, and
Father was a shadow to Mother's giant.

Later Father became the giant, Mother became
his shadow and we no longer believed in God.

The author's bloodshot eye peered into the window
of a dollhouse and the doll died from fright.

Culture inlaid with lapis lazuli, set in a
Victorian pendant, passed down until auctioned.

In this chapter, Mother lives in a glass box
nestled in satin, Father in a cedar cubbyhole,

Korean characters, like stiff phonetic Legos,
wait to join with one another while

St. Jerome writes with his single eyelash quill
in his painfully exact studio.

# Body Builder

I can no longer blush.  Half-face towards the starchy scape.
Birds limn the spindle trees, their Listerine-hued eyes dart
as they trill mechanical dirges tabulating not again, not
again / I can no longer blush. The flat arctic sky
boundlessly jogs to another hemisphere / She grows!
Or her pectoral grows or all her pectorals grow / A drop of body
oil the size of a water balloon splooshes down on a man as a graceless
anointing, atomizing into tears / How delicate the sounds are from
her height! Glottal roses wink out of their throats:  their voices
tine/ Now I am blushing / Swamp moss draped over the arcades / *Oh
she'll topple. She's making for the welkin* / swamps massage
the plywood foundations of our houses / And speaking of / she shoots
up not like a beanstalk but a city erected quick-time / and speaking
of, I blush blood / Roiling up past 200 ft, dizzy from all that phosphagen / *I
be damned where she gits all that nylon, the size of wedding tents!*/ She
flexes for her audience / Naugahide.  Fuel injection. A sawed-off
shotgun will do you nothing just the rat-a-tat-tat / Rabelaisian
bullhonkies hunker and tinker tents around her / Roiling,
flexing / *are louts without a law to bless them* / a shadow
overcast / a footstep is a swamp in which gators pop up like whack-
a-mole carnival games / what are they saying? do they marvel?/ *I am
hemorrhaging flames!* / she aims with her thumb.

# Melanin

Here is the world; I lost the world or so I thought;

Here is the wind, the weather of winds,
poplar trees beating air, pages lifted and scattered,

lesions growing to consonants, and a woman
with iguanas wreathed around her hair;

She followed fair Confession home
and copied her, without leaving smudges.

Here is the wind, the weather of wind,
wind chimes colliding in a minor haunted key,

a lone shawl cartwheeling, tattered, contagious;
a Vietnamese pieta, Madonna with eyes like asterisks

and a smudgy mouth; a flenser with rubber boots
who skinned a whale, a goat, an angel.

Here is a coiffured sham who leaned forward
in the wind and moaned.

Here is the world; I lost the world or so I thought;
I toweled my face,

expecting it to flake off like dirt worms
to reveal a bright white skull. I loved her

with a flawed body and in the morning hologram
my shameful tears slid down her thighs

Here is the wind that uprooted the lands,
tar pits overflowed, smeared the debutante hairs.

Wind cut away at sandstone cliffs to carve
a boxing ring and then the wind paused,

Pale crustaceous men skittered down to see
the fight and were surprised to see the lone

pugilist, a dark-skinned woman who spat
and sparred, who keeled forward,

kissed canvas with her teeth,
and rose again.

# Assimilation of Sitting

I.

in this house, there are only shallow tables,

littered with glasses, liquor the color of chrome, industry,
or it's more volatile than that:

the way alcohol flickers with the blue glare of television,
dissolving it to a spent image:

lanterns floating, bulbs harvesting a hesitant path
through water, creeks, rivers,

where soiled laundry and occasional deaths
have found their plangent plots,

And then the disruption of a hand or hands—

each glass emptied, refilled, emptied again,
paltry or fat lips swilling, masculine lips,

the last scatterings of anju, appetizers,
the shavings of cuttlefish—

these are the men in the narrative,
the few women who interrupt—

sitting around the floors, mulberry or linoleum,
the positioning of mats after labor,

being privy to other rumors, other lives,
throne, mat, the courier that exacts a proper name.

II.

claim the putti, the secondhand Fragonard,
to make respect is to frame the house,

wood gold, threadless brocade, a Steinway—
the mimicry of motorized sonatas,

property is still shrink-wrapped,
the gilded age has the scent of sesame,

the goosed-up seats are unweathered,
we prefer to squat,

squat to pickle vegetables, squat to fry sesame

living room as altar, couch excised,
post seamstress, post factory, post facto.

III.

though the drill caught his shin,
father developed metal catarrh,

and turned his children to letterings,
quarantined—

canter, the western saddle, the plywood chair,
neck pulleyed upwards,

mouth wringing dictation, ironically
it was a Filipino teacher who would

not let us out until our spine
was a suspended fishing wire.

I used those same chairs
to straddle a learned man and later

a learned woman, both their feet
pointed downwards

like Cinderella when the shoe fit.

IV.

Our illuminated manuscript is the kneel,
the mat no longer secular

but bridal white, distilled by maxims,
the obsessive dustings by my mother—

The mats are specialized,

I have seen people kneel on that cold-cut
cushioning, rubbing their oak beads,

I have seen it stacked like the winner's side
in checkers, or piles of unopened envelopes,

I have stood and looked up at these
once functional mats behind glass,

shoplifted by anthropologists,

but sitting on them, I am aware of
my spine, my tailbone,

I would rather sit on the ground,
it is safer, less slippery

or give it to an ancestor who needs a rest—

she is out of breath
from spanning our labor of crossing.

**II.**

# The Shameful Show of Tono Maria

Exhibit a: The girl and/or a girl.

Exhibit b: Drenching heat from a bleak sun.
A black gold–flecked body beneath a gown thin
as a Flemish veil.

Exhibit c: My mouth opened and closed
like a guppy. Verbs were lost, ellipses
trailed off like dregs.

Exhibit d: In 1810, an American audience
wiped their sweating napes and waited
with vinegary desire.

Exhibit e: Still mute, I was sent to Special Ed
with autistics, paraplegics, and a boy
who only ate dirt.

Exhibit f: Before her show: a man who was
only a torso and head. Propped on a pedestal,
he would smoke a cigarette between the barker's
two fingers.

Exhibit g: She was from an Indian tribe
in Brazil. She liked whiskey, puzzles, and
generous men. She used lanolin on her burn scars.

Exhibit h: Later in college, I drank bourbon,
slurred out swears. I was suspicious that some
man I slept with was an Asiaphile.

Exhibit i: The barker stressed the number
of her scars and called her a *savage Mary Magdalene*.

Exhibit j: I pinched my throat's skin to remember
last night's act. Guilt as throat as torso.

Exhibit k: She peeled off her gown and bared her body
graphed with 134 scars. One scar for each time
she committed adultery, punished by her own tribe.

Exhibit l: the girl and/or a girl as the hyperbolic secret.

Exhibit m: A man asked *how much for your hide?*
Standing on the platform, she shoved his face
away with her nude foot.

Exhibit n: the girl and/or a girl brings her palms
together, mimes repentance.

Exhibit o: As they gawked at the 134 scars
of her insatiable lust, she closed her eyes and counted
until the numbers dissolved into her homeland:
the ocean with its black coral reef, a lover
she preferred, the burns she never grew numb to.

Exhibit p: She opened her eyes and smiled.
She plucked favors from each gaping mouth.

# During Bath

I am an old man in my fantasies, a darting pupil, a curious ghost.

Two catacombic bodies: legs, arms, salamander
tongues, their skin is fair.

Sometimes they are in a field colored by autumn,
a garden knitted by cabbage, stakes of fat tomatoes.

Sun that marks their leonine shapes—
the scent of cunt and lemon verbena.

Now it is just me in a large room with all the dolls
I used to own, stacked like bags of flour.

Or in the bath, taking the shape of Marat.
Arm slung over the ledge edge like iced fish,

water that is less warm, a sideshow shadow,
my own darker skin.

The tongue to mid-palate. Coiled to the back of your teeth,
tighten your throat muscle. Utter a low pitch, exhale.

There is no room to exhale.

My parents did not moan or even breathe for fear
of waking their children.

Palpitation, cyst, polyp: skin licked,
tongue pioneers along topographic pulp.

Why is it only words that I think of?
It is not my hand that touches his face, but a hand,

the mark on his face does not last a second
though I want it to singe.

To first write the words:
undressed, blueprint, revolver.

Return to the bath: the loaves of my breasts, navel,
blood rush. I am not anemic. Repeat

rose, fuck, paean: to first write the words.

# All the Aphrodisiacs

blowfish arranged on a saucer. Russian roulette. angelic slivers.

ginseng. cut antlers allotted in bags dogs on a spit, a Dutch girl

winking holds a bowl of shellfish.

white cloth, drunkenness. a different language leaks out—
the idea of throat, an orifice, a cord—

you say it turns you on when I speak Korean.

The gold paste of afterbirth, no red—

Household phrases     —*pae-go-p'a*  *(I am hungry)*
                         —*ch'i-wa*    *(Clean up)*
                         —*kae sekki*  *(Son of a dog)*

I breathe those words in your ear, which make you climax;

afterwards you ask me for their translations. I tell you it's a secret.

*gijek niin tigit rril*—the recitation of the alphabet; guttural diphthong, gorgeous.

What are the objects that turn me on: words—

*han-gul*: the language first used by female entertainers, poets, prostitutes.

The sight of shoes around telephone wires, pulleyed by their laces, the
        blunt word cock.

Little pink tutus in FAO Schwarz,
when I was four they used to dress me as a boy,

white noise, whitewashed. the whir of ventilation in the library.

Even quarantined amongst books, I tried to kiss you once.

Strips of white cotton, the color of the commoner, the color of virtue,
the color that can be sullied—

my hand pressed against your diaphragm, corralling your pitch,

a pinch of rain caught between mouths,

analgesic, tea. poachers drawing blood—

strips of white cotton I use to bind your wrist to post, tight
enough to swell vein, allow sweat—

sweat to sully the white of your sibilant body,

the shrug of my tongue, the shrug of command, *ssshhht.*

# Not Henry Miller but Mother

Passion is the letter "p." A jeweled pear, another Guernica shattering our souls, a giant liced with Lilliputians. Passion fell flat on its face when a date used too much tongue. Passion ran, shotput into the air past the score-board, past the empty lots where children brawled silently, past the mani-cured lawns of Silicon Valley's royalty and past my sweaty, consumptive grasp. Following the flock, I traveled to Europe and scaled the Catalan steps to view a landscape of stone. It was cold. I left early. Later in Paris, I searched for passion in the vessel of a Frenchman and only found a janitor who cleaned the toilets of Notre Dame and whispered "I have many, many flaws." She was the one who hoarded passion. Mother, who shaved my head when I was three, who dieted on tears and Maalox, who shouted in hyena rage and one minute later cradled my face and whispered a song in my ear, while I watched the clock in front of me, ticking.

# On Splitting

Wind does not whip, it caresses. Or it whips when a mail order song crescendos in the background. The blowsy sails. The fat, fat sky.

We blow air bubbles. Once they touch the dry outer skin of your lips, they pop: a pocket of unsaid gas.

The taste of body, the drumming on lard. A kind of love that has become autistic.

Mother and Father on the hilt of a sugary cake. An avalanche but a minor one that tastes confectionery. Photographs of Mother the bride. A stiff smile that does not like dairy.

Denote passion.

A Korean wedding. There is a sign for blushing: two perfect red circles pasted on the bride's cheeks. Or it's a sign for passion, good luck, or maybe it's to hide the pallor.

The girl takes the knife, the boy takes it from her, the girl takes the knife, the boy takes it from her, the girl takes the knife, the boy takes it from her, the girl takes the knife, the boy takes it from her.

The stage is set for the woman with the killer whale eyes. She announces, 'there is no love, only longing.'

My mother said, "If you eat lying down , you'll grow hair on your crotch."

To find passion, I should have written a lyric poem. A poem that would roll off the tongue like icing, curdles curds , whey, icing, a cube of ice.

The first Korean man I liked shared a plate of squid with me. I called him brother because I was much younger than he. Chewing on a flank, he told me he'd slept with five women and fallen in love with one.

I grew a petri dish of princes, all replicating and jostling each other for my hand.

Afterwards, we kissed in the dark enclaves of a stuffy TV room. Our tongues were not sure of each other and our breaths stank of salted squid. It was not what I fantasized.

I am here to lick your shoes, your hairy shins, your eventual cock.

My parents never kissed in public. Except once. An obligation on the cheek before my father left.

The word most often said during lovemaking: *ttagawu*. This could mean itchy or spicy. The same word used when wearing a wool sweater that irritates, or easing into a tub of scalding water.

I would have preferred a sealed letter, even a terse message taped to the refrigerator. Rather than the talk, the awkwardness of it, the restraint. *A letter daggers her heart* — dagger. The histrionics of dagger.

To restrain.

Adolescent obsessions: Greek mythology, heavy metal rock stars, documentation of freaks (Mexican midget, triplets, albino sword swallowers), iron-on T-shirts, breasts, he who gave you your first bong hit and kiss.

Along the soldered road, he lies motionless. I arrive and crouch down. Kiss his rigor mortis lips and he rises. This is a holy scripture or a movie.

We barely knew each other yet he confessed to me until his face clattered off like a hubcap.

Restraint turns passion into shame. Or worse, martyrs. My mother comes from a country of martyrs, a fetish of martyrs, a crateful of martyrs.

This is not a precious jade bracelet. It is plastic, given to me by my Italian friend who bought it for 50 cents.

The girl takes the knife.

I don't know the Korean word for sex. I ask Mother, Father, a couple of aunts. What's the word? They feign ignorance. I ask a friend living in Seoul. Even she doesn't know. "There are many words that refer to it. Just not one definite one."

Along the soldered road, there is a man sleeping. I pause, wanting to kiss him. But I am apprehensive that he would awake, become offended or confused. I shut the book or I open the book, earmark the page, shut the book.

# Movement

(I said) hello
(I said) blue adds to maelstrom

(Vines wove wildly around the window
the way damp flannel sheets roiled around our
sweaty legs, our faces stiff as caulk)

(you said)   how your strobe light moods
           flashed while winds

sprouted like weeds, while we sucked juice
from matronly oranges.

(Those vines became elegiac eels, leafless
and insinuating. While drunk)

I wanted your neck. (Flighty altitude in
a shallow room, tongues flapping

for attention. A nosebleed while lovemaking.

Blood rind. Letters in hiatus. I cupped all
your facial bones in one palm.)

Aphasia during crisis or mouth to mouth,
kiss as confession's replica,

(I asked for noise) you played
(I asked again) and then you paused.

# Translating Michin'yun

Gorgon, lost hysteric. Marsupial men in blue tiaras.

She picked off the last flakes of herself: organs,
crumbs, inflatable trousers.

Drinking rice wine along the Han River, we talked
about this sexual revolution, the good girls
who give fellatio in karaoke rooms.

*Mich*-bitch-in-a-house-box-bed shattered by sound.

He blamed Korea's promiscuity on Japan:
"We carelessly fuck around like those imperialists."

Old-fashioned vibrators used as cures for hysterics.

I spoke mindlessly: Nest of mosquitoes. Fat man with gout. Caw.

The husband or father who uses it as insult or banter.

If hot-tempered, if having affairs, if too cerebral, if—

Used too commonly: "Michin'yun is late."
Melancholic dial tone. Throat sags monastically, fattens to a curse.

Sallow, raving, she returned to the village after four years
of work (what she did or where she worked, no one knew.)

# To Collage a Beginning

I.

*to begin*

I always drew the face first

large eyes, blond locks, thimble lips

and broad streaks across canvas, the scent
of cold cream, paper thick as cloth napkins

I noticed a blond shepherdess
who ate sushi out of a wicker basket

The way a story began, the rich lining
of a first sentence, how we worship clarity

the curtains rising to a startling chronology,
rays jutting like stalactite, a projection

in a wet blue cathedral—I wanted
to start a conversation over again with my father

in airbrushed light over coffee,
when we weren't worn or tired—

No one could not remember my first word,
it could have been *oma*, *appa*, *bap*, *uyu* or

*home, friend*, it could have been sex, the first
English word I taught my immigrant cousin

which he repeated over and over like a child—

II.

*to land*

Gasp at the first sight

of an amusement park, the prickly

circle of a Ferris wheel swooping down—

a small girl with a white hat draws
poignant circles on the unmarked sand—

how luxurious it would be to write poetry
about unpeopled landscape,

rolling hills, the fog winding over a silhouette
of spruce trees, a pond iced over and air,

sharp high altitude air, clinging to my chest
already tarred by a glaze of ink—

Once the gatherer landed
she saw small blue flags marking every half-mile—

(My grandmother once had a Japanese surname.
Women were sent to coal mines to work shirtless)

I dreamed of glaciers marked with graffiti,
a waiting room cutting through the first place I lived.

III.

*to desire*

a huge fuchsia department store called *sampoong bekajum* (Gift)

collapsed one day, killing hundreds of women who were

browsing through dresses, baskets of oranges, and mackerel—

after the wreckage was cleared, there was a blank plot of land
and a naked woman who whirled around in a circle—

holding nothing but chanting I want I want I want.

IV.

*to dress*

they soaped and clothed her in a high-necked dress
with a bustle to make her lucid—

*she tracked in mud, her cunt was in flames,* they said.

I wanted petticoats and blue-white hair, the blue
was so startling, it made me cry *so new, so wonderfully new!*

To name the native, you must first dress her

when they undressed her at night, they found
hoarded manifestos taped to her flesh—

she expected origami white underneath her flaking
skin but it was peacock blue and black

what are the first words, she asked her father and—

imported for her exaggerated ass—

shed her old dust-ridden pelt, left her hut and oil fire

what are the first words, she asked her father and—

I was not afraid to undress in front of her,
it was a used dress, an ill-fitting dress.

V.

*to listen*


*Chapsuseyo*: beef slats clothed in lettuce, griddled
vowels, hostess puckered thank you in a breath
(how do you bow, how do you
say *eat* formally)—winding spiral stairs
lead to ears that lead
to verbs tiered for a higher
and wider

*Mich-inyun*: exiled from the table
but I've already left, Korean soap operas, infidel's
broken foot, jaundiced from the attic,
burn the hoop, the act, the barker's
dictating laugh, bedlam!
But little was heard,
feckless woman
—how could

*Malsum*: what what? said the daft old man,
whose hearing aid was crushed by his family
who *mums* the word—swallowed words,
anxieties—portrait of my forensic thumb,
singing I fly, I want, I need—Listen to the native's
monologue, listen as you would when
your footsteps are echoed by another—
Raid a brothel of philosophers!
You need a helmet,
some wings, sheets of rain—
it was a fresh beginning
over such noise! It was—

**III**.

# Hottentot Venus

Overheard in the heat, the air, the fruit fly's drone
of the perfect helix, overheard in science's repartee

of right and wrong, in the gossip of perfumed women
basking in London's charmless sun,

Overheard in the gasps of penny sideshows, the formulas
of doctors summing up freaks in taxidermic clinics,

Overheard in the echo of cubic hallways,
in the speculum's wand first tested on the slave woman,

Overheard in history's senile tympanum

was a Song.

*Rain irrigating fact, jars mapping name,*
*Recollect my throat, my organs, my bones*

★

Overheard was the scribble of a biologist's notes,
the showman's bark of choreographed answers:

*(4'6" ¹/₂, 98 lb., skin tone is a jaundiced yellow brown)*
She stepped to the right, she stepped to the left,

*(thighs measure 4" deep in the back, 1" in the front)*
She lumbered forward, she lumbered backwards,

*(face is remarkably simian: a flat nose .5" from tip to septum)*
She pushed out her lower lip, furrowed her brows

*(The mouth is wide and flat, 1.7" in width)*
She danced to the hurdy gurdy, shuffling back and shuffling forth

*(Most spectacular is the sheer width of her buttocks)*
And then she turned her back to the audience,

*(Suffering from Steatopygia, her buttocks are 9" deep in fat)*
She heard the titters of the crowd as they drew nearer,

*(2 hemispherical cushions of fat that come to an apex)*
"The size of a whale!" "A sink!" "A cauldron pot!"

*(and slopes down near her savage genitals.)*
A parasoled woman poked, a mustachioed man fondled,

*(her moods are erratic, often disagreeable)*
She sighed as they poked with their very own hands,

*(and her sexual appetite rapacious)*
and desired ardor, enlightenment, an ermine coat.

★  ★

A ragged trail of rain leaked through
the cracked stubble of my apartment ceiling,

and was beating down on the dozen laid-out pots
when the Hottentot Venus arrived at my home

and spoke with quiescence and rage:

*What a piece of work is man that*
*a servant girl from South Africa was bartered*

*from showman to doctor, from doctor to showman.*
*I died from the cold and from the hands of these doctors.*

*And still they used my rotted body to show*
*What-a-piece-of-work-is-man.*

The rain ceased its drumming. Clouds tugged
apart and drifted, canvassing

each window with their idle shadows.
She turned to me and asked:

*And why have you resurrected me?*
as a symbol, an allegory, a mirror image of myself?

*We are the stone reliefs of men in their chariots,*
*the fat trimmed off classification.*

I dreamed that I kissed a lion's maw
and pulled fat from my breast like taffy,

burning down childhood pageants where I
was the slant-eyed jester in a shapeless gown

*They called me the Missing Link, though*
*I knew Dutch, English, a little bit of French*

watching the parabola of onlookers watching
the autopsied body

*They impounded me with their cold intentions*

(the doctors viewed the spook that
she tucked behind her apron)

dreamed of their butcher paper, their incising
each border: mouth, vulva and eyelid.

*Once, London's sun was darker than*
*dead coal and I bit my tongue like an epileptic.*

Overheard the hissing world, cold rain,
and a tale that burned in its preamble:

*You who number and plot:*
*honor your gilded canes, your portrait ladies.*
*I tear you apart as I have been torn.*

★   ★   ★

# Androgynous Pronoun

(*nakshil*) the sound of fishing.    (*o-rak*) play.

(*ga-ul*) suit knitted from leaves colored cumin and cayenne.

(*ip*) mandible.    (*ip damu*) mandible slew.

(*ko*) I inherited my father's nose.    (*ku'rum*) also his walk.

(*want*) pronounced won-ha-da.  won-ha-da wooed

a flat-chested woman.    her arms enfolded.

Hers puddled between her legs.    His streamed past twenty fences.
(*She said she was a man. He challenged her to a piss*)

(*mip'ta*) rattling stomach  (*yep-u-da*) bloated legs

The custom of the hermaphrodite cut perfectly in half.

Body like a balloon inflated by asthmatic breath.

The hirsute man twirled around, became Bette Davis.

(*kunyun*) a soldier's armpits.  (*kunyun*) tangerine robes.

Hermaphrodite twirls to switch again, but trips in between.

# The Scavenging

There is no order; no primary triads,
no grids or echoing radii

but an asylum—carnation, crane white,
bouquets of lurid pink clowns and holy apostles

patterned on muslin, voile or Titian silk,
fabrics used to wrap and hold

her things, fat bundles that are now
hoarded—my source, my humiliation.

I am hungry for cloth,
sweat's stain from travel and labor.


Once I sewed fifty white seat cushions,
self-effaced, the washboard of final gauze

into flattened seats for an audience, where
I performed body holding body,

distilling the maelstrom of moods —
objects, carnation, crane white,

bouquets of faces that stared while I stole
words, men, an audience of holy apostles

or leering clowns, and the claps or the cane
used to yank away the freak who

can only speak through *things*,
the invention of cloth and the motion of needle.

Her wrappings hold the stench of rationed
anchovies, the tension of Japanese surnames,

the revolution of Molotov cocktails
with their throaty flames, the blast of patriotism.

But these are guesses based on historians
who call Korea poor country, who poeticize

about night soil and human shit—she has never
unknotted her gathered *bottaris*

except the scrap bag which only held skins
and that one story, repeated over and over—

the 38th parallel, the sons already south,
she and her daughters the last to cross.

She carried too many bundles, unknotting them
to take out a frame or dish and leave it behind,

not knowing there was a scavenger
who pawned her objects for exemption.

# CAT Scan

I will stroll through

negative space molded in blubber.  Dildo interior.    Gurney

waiting like a bobbed tongue.    Neurons        caseworkers

marching through fiberglass.    A keen-eyed

tourist.    a battery of cameras f-stops a heart and a brain

Okra electric.   Bring on the whitening loofah

the paint by number schemata      my ideals, my love

Old-world love!       Body electric my tantric ass.

Again that clicking       a riff guitar flayed, bar coded:

A night in your spare, poised room.      Rise, rise, I will rise

context a soliloquy on dole       just me shrink-wrapping air.

I won't wait for that nest of minutiae—

Oxtails, donuts, a morning regret. A rewired booth will

predict my synaptic sparring, my early dawn

special in lite-brite fusillade.   Here, an impeccable

map, a turnstile revolving, the last confessional

before I'm out your door, your illegible pod.

# Wing 1

It was a season when green was not a mnemonic green. A butterfly was bludgeoned by sight or a careless fist. Hazy light was light seen through tears and light for the wedding was hazy. Smelly carnations, doily-rimmed cake. There was no one in attendance except the gold-frocked pastor and my father. Even the groom did not show (my father grabbed him prowling along the sidewalk, declaring, "Here, a Korean man! The perfect DNA!") First daughter watched the procession with a peach-colored RSVP in hand. The box was checked "No, I cannot attend—but I will watch, eat cake, and tap my shoes." Seasons changed. Memory was pixilated when faced with meadow and space. Air accelerated to wind, ideal for aviation. My father sent a videotape and diagram, showing how the wedding should be planned, and saw her figure weaving in the air before the plunge: Frigid gale whipping feathers, hoarded phrases, trained words, home-bound vernaculars (he cried *udi-ru ga!*), the sump of romanized words now an alloy, a compromise.

# Wing 2 (Secret Language of Home Exposed)

hills   piss   barley  tea
fly  rolling  high spell eczema a
tongue  coated  blue  rag  washing
it  tantrum shrill  thickets

hills
piss barley tea fly rolling high spell
eczema a tongue coated blue
rag washing it tantrum
shrill thickets the

hillspiss
barleyteaflyrollinghigh
spelleczemaatonguecoatedbluerag
washingittantrumthicketsthehill

# Wing 3 (Secret Language of Home Exposed)

udi  ru  ga  moyok
he    jigum  kuk  jinma
di  sajimi  musun  omma
haggi  shi-ru  gaji  ma  ya  gaji


udi ru ga moyok
he jigum kuk jinma
di sajimi musun omma
haggi shi-ru gaji ma ya gaji


udirugamoyok
hejigumkukjinma
disajimimusunomma
haggishi-rugajimayagaji

# Wing 4

As light, as elocution, as game, as mnemonic game,
the twin card of that tulip is on the right,
the twin card of that girl is on the left,
The homonym of capitol is capital, accept is except
allude is elude, rain is reign is rein,
the homonym of weather is whether
cite is sight is site, there is sideshow.
I fell in the line of fire between a tourist's camera
and site. Grew hair until it grew on my face,
the rabbit is the Marlboro man,
the house with the cool, Mediterranean tiles
is along the California tundra.
The twin card of horse is below,
the twin card of bell is above,
"Wings should be made of saddles
and etiquette," my father said
"Be grateful for story's intention," my teacher said.
I used to walk out of the classroom halfway through
story time be dragged back by the ear.
The twin card of bird is right behind, adjacent,
the twin card of book is right of way,
twin card of plane is mobile, all throughout,
fear that airplanes would soar past the papery stars
and collide with the globe's glass ceiling,
fear of all that was finite.
Site of an empty school lot. Cited in a book erased of story
but no sight of wings being rebuilt,
only the suggestion of wings,
the first words uttered,
a hapless face bloated with exhibitionist dreams.

# Ablution

As if I wrote myself
to a sparkling erasure,

or spoke with the wooden
clack of a puppet's mouth,

my palimpsest face haggard
from revision,

obsession for a glassblower's
perfection the way a pianist

obsesses: her fingers spidering
so fast down a scale she bursts into flames.

Or the folk singer who sings until she
coughs blood so that her voice will be
transcendent.

As if you did not ask for enough tears.
Never sleeping, always enduring:

Art that is a room so white it's blue,
and a copy of Kant by the hospital bed.

Limbs were as unyielding as a whale's fin,
and the mind burned white

in a Korean bathhouse, where there were
no Degas dancers but women

with flaccid breasts scrubbing
their bodies like the casual chore

of scrubbing laundry. Throwing
buckets of scalding water over themselves

to wash away the dirt that could
break out in worms.

All around there was the violence of steam
to clean, clean, to clean

as you wove on your loom
anathema and gift for your departure.

# The Gatherer

she has landed: a treatise of hair, a parachute
which she wears as suit, a flame suit that tails out
for miles, cowling the land that is hoary
and new—

      Landed in:
an island without the slur of trees that fan
into peacock of sugar canes
used for capital and switch.
It is an island that no one wants.
No economy—only the grainy fog,
the watery sky, the linted
exhaust of land.

When I think of her,
I wonder how she keeps company,
what is her language, does she speak
to herself, sing, give monologues?
Does she go insane, swallow her tongue,
having no receiver, no catcher except
the bald landscape—the watery sky?
Does she unpeel?

I only know the sketch of her hands—
the close-up of fist, the gathering
the phonetic of hands:

The compass of wrist and the ball
of her palm,
the cords of her veins
that curl down to gather air.
Bending over to pick up the idea of object.
The ballet of fingers that pinches off a bud
of 'fern.' She digs for 'root,'
the head of 'fish,' along with the effort of mime,
the atom of sweat.

This is all I know. Her figure is muddled
by parachute and she breathes as if
between two words. I can only translate
her gestures—the syntax of pathos
is lost, along with the glossary
of character.

But as the solitary tenant and colony,
I can tell you her gestures promote
the yearning for a kiss,
the last of a prelude, a title.
She is mine, and I her object,
searching for our imagined core.

# Translating Mo'um

## *mo'um 1:*

the utterance is an alm, the deep palaver of monk,
the demure lips—the struggle to speak with a mouth full
of water without spilling, the *mmm*
the hurried *um*, an afterthought, ghost, as if
embarrassed to say—

mo'um is:
>       fur
>           food
>               heart
>                   lust

or changing my mind, it is none of this:

>           mother always asked me: *mo'umi a-p'a?*

And it is *fever* that I first defined as mo'um,
the chills, heated energy—

>           *oma ujiruh* (Mother, I am dizzy)

>               fevers whose gift was a day off from school,
>               my blanket a thermostat, hothouse avalanche,

>           *sagwa moguh* (Eat this apple)

to cool off the thick-lensed heat,
mother offered me peeled fruit, sliced in sweet geometry

>           I answered: *Mo'umi appa oma.*

Fever is the pathology of blushing,
knotted heat, red shrouding sight,

the dull fat tongue, throb of bone hugging muscle.
All I wanted to do was sleep, to leave this body,

to ache like the memory of acupuncture needles
perched around Grandmother's throat

*(ch'im maju*—which means spit but also
the hot blend of needles used to exorcise

as if mo'um was spirit, steam, leashed dog—
never the opaque doll but the battery that ran it.)

Grandmother kneeled. Two whorls against the floor:
the difference between mo'um and ma'hum,

always the pain that we first associate with mo'um,
the weight of fist to breast.

To associate mo'um with action:

    to forsake
       to hide
         to cleanse
           to transcend

One by one, each house caught on fire and
burned down. We saw no flames, only smoke

bellying out of windows, the ash that rained
and darkened our skins, the martyr naked by the window,

a spotlight on her as she waited for the flames to catch.

How easy is it to slough body, as if it is a sock, pennies,
the folktales of wells and filial daughters,

For the bread she gave up though she was starving,
the daughter ascends in a blue-white gown.

While she ascends, there are floodlights that declare
her image, strokes of watercolor: flaxen, rose, white

always the erasing white: white curtains, stairs,

gowns folded in rows, and women bound in white,
crying, each tear carrying away a morsel of skin

(I was in the corner, taking water from their tears
and rubbing them on my cheeks as my camouflage.)

# *mo'um 2:*

(The women's quarters in the Chos'on Dynasty were tucked away behind the spring, south of a rocky footpath. They slipped around as if there was nothing but air behind their silk dresses. One day, a frustrated wife, wearing only her underdress, ran out to the front gate and slapped her unfaithful husband with a bag of grains that was the weight of flesh. She was the cautionary figure.)

(While mother prayed during communion, I would sneak tastes of her wine and, break off pieces of her bread and slip them in my mouth, letting them melt on my tongue because it was so thin. The bread was forbidden to children. It was delicious.)

(The bell tongue of Sundays, the dogs that poke their muzzles through the diamonds of chain-link fences, the gathering of migrants to first repent and then eat.)

(Dark-eyed body, simian woman. That night, ash fell like feathers before coating one's skin, water gathered in a fist. I waited before cleaning myself.)

(I borrow the mo'um by sliding off my clothes, fondling, swallowing hard to feel the girth of throat.)

## mo'um 3:

I took the gold, the ventriloquist's voice, the locks of hair, took

the code, the breasts, the lush vowel, and the infinitive

that could suit anyone (to eat, to suckle, to lust, to drink, to come,

to wash, to speak, to touch, to fuck, to speak. I have spoken, I have

spoken earnestly, I have lied.) I took the body. Snatched it, the one in the

left-hand corner; it is huddling, dancing, it does not move. Or clawed away

at the dark green soil, to the stone box where she lay, and took hers—

I took glossaries, the lucid mouth, singing birds

by the wings, I took in secret, with soiled hands

since I forgot to wash before meals, or wipe away the sleep from my eyes,

or clean between my legs and clean off the ash that has powdered

my skin. She claps in the background when I

plunge into the pool into a canopy of bubbles and water that lifts,

explode to the clarity of air and the mo'um that sings.

# Timetable

girl slur vessel 1,9,8,0, plot mangled

lode inflection of a face bleeding patter

a bowl nailed to wood   a hand caught in air

(brindled body trapped, a room pocked with drains)

*il, eeh, sam, sah*   sweet plum by the machine

slum run rank   I mangled intaglio tense

(We hid our excess arms and horns, hemmed our suits,

sheared our hair, haunted an inch of this room )

water water   said said   hand wringing sob

squids strung to dry *shoo shoo*   black onion stink

hire 800 for 8 tables said calligraphic slang

(No time to talk, no time to fuck, no time to piss, no)

freeze-dried communion   wet slip of sheet

he walked on pennies held together by molasses

(we gathered and dispersed   gathered, dispersed)

the ship stowing 200 capsized   molting to a coral reef

a place to sit   a place for exposure

the lights at the end of the shore are red.

# Notes

**Hottentot Venus:** Originally from the San tribe in South Africa, Saartje Baartman was exhibited in England for her overdeveloped buttocks and genitalia. After her deat, her preserved labia and skeleton were displayed in the Musee de l'Homme. She was billed as the Hottentot Venus.

**Translating *Mo'um*:** The standard Romanized spelling of *Mo'um* is *Mom*.